THE LAKE DISTRICT

AND SURROUNDING SPLENDOUR

CUMBRIA: A COUNTY OF CONTRASTS

Cumbria is huge; among English counties only North Yorkshire is larger. It encompasses the bulge of land bounded by Morecambe Bay and the Solway Firth, takes in part of the Yorkshire Dales National Park and borders Scotland for some twenty miles. Almost half its border is shoreline, with miles of extensive sandy beaches, wide estuaries, dunes and mudflats, which are havens for birds and other wildlife. From the coast the land rises quickly to the high fells of Lakeland, but the southern peninsulas of Furness and Cartmel have gentler hills and valleys, and the Solway Plain, in the north, is positively flat. The River Eden runs through the heart of the county, and much of its sixty-five-mile journey from the Yorkshire Dales to its mouth at the Solway Firth is through a peaceful green valley, cut through the limestone crags of the Dales and moorland of the north Pennines.

A whitewashed, stone-built farmhouse near Ulpha, in the southern lakes

Rushbearing parade, Ambleside

TRADITIONS AND ACTIVITIES

Traditional ways of life and a genuine Cumbrian identity have survived twentieth-century pressures, and there are countless regional customs and events throughout the year. These include the sports of fell running, Lakeland wrestling and hound trailing. The county's museums include the Windermere Steamboat Museum, the Stott Park Bobbin Mill and Tullie House in Carlisle. There are waterborne pursuits of rowing, yachting and windsurfing, or the more passive pastime of taking a steamboat on Coniston Water. Opportunities for fell-walking are endless, or you can simply meander leisurely through some of the most spectacular scenery in the world.

Sheep form the backbone of Cumbria's agricultural economy

The Windermere Steamboat Museum at Bowness

Boats tied to the jetty at Ambleside

TEMPERATE SHORES AND RUGGED HILLS

CARTMEL AND FURNESS PENINSULAS

Cumbria's southern peninsulas, Cartmel to the east and Furness to the west, extend like stubby fingers into the shifting sands of Morecambe Bay. Inland the scenery is characterised by rugged hills, rising to the Furness Fells lying between the southern ends of Windermere and Coniston. The coast, fringed by extensive sands, is indented by the wide, peaceful estuaries of the Duddon, Leven and Kent rivers which are a paradise for birds. Grange-over-Sands, in the sheltered Leven estuary, is the region's main resort, dubbed the Cumbrian Riviera and reputed to have the highest spring-time temperature in the north of England.

Historically the peninsulas were dominated by the religious houses which bore their names – but the remains of Cartmel Priory and Furness Abbey are only two of many interesting historical sites in the region. Stately homes open to the public include Holker Hall, Levens Hall and Sizergh Castle.

Island fortress

Tiny Piel Island, off the lonely southernmost tip of Cumbria, is only half a mile across, but it houses a castle, a bird reserve, seven cottages and a pub, the Ship Inn. Amenities are few – there is no electricity on the island and access is by boat from Roa Island or by tractor across the sands from Walney Island – but the atmosphere is magical. The ruined castle, never much more than a single pele tower, was built by the monks of Furness to protect their shipping from Scots raiders.

Stronghold of the Stricklands

Everything at Sizergh Castle is the work of the Strickland family, who have lived here since 1239. Like so many great Cumbrian houses, the present building began as a fourteenth-century pele tower; subsequent additions maintained its air of formidable strength. In Tudor times much expense was lavished on the building, resulting in Sizergh's chief glory, its splendidly carved interior woodwork.

Decorative support

The choir stalls of St Mary's, Cartmel, contain some splendidly ornate misericords – hinged seats which when tipped up have a ledge to support standing clergy. As this fine example illustrates, each ledge is elaborately carved with biblical or allegorical scenes.

An English country house

Originally a thirteenth-century pele tower, Levens Hall has remained substantially unaltered since the eighteenth century. It has all the charm of an English country house – oak panelling, elaborate plasterwork, antiques and huge chimneys – but its most memorable feature is the extraordinary topiary garden, laid out in 1694. Since then it has grown into a surreal array of oversize, fantastic, green sculptures.

Low water at Bardsea

The outgoing tide leaves the wide sands at Bardsea exposed and gleaming in the grey evening light. Here the sea bites into the south Cumbrian coast, and across the waters of the Leven estuary the Cartmel peninsula is dimly visible. The coast at Bardsea is lined with ancient woodland, once Crown property and planted with oaks for ships' timbers, but now a pleasant country park.

Religious power base

The great arcade of Furness Abbey's chapter house forms the most impressive of its extensive ruins. In its time the abbey was the second richest Cistercian house in the country after Fountains Abbey, and it ruled the Furness peninsula as though it were an independent state, acquiring land as far afield as the Isle of Man and even Ireland.

Raceday at Cartmel

When the races come to Cartmel twice a year the village is shaken out of its usual tranquil existence, becoming a bustling hub of activity. Hundreds of people throng the stalls and rails of the racecourse. Set in superb parkland, it is one of the most attractive in the country.

Comedy's kings live on

The world's only Laurel and Hardy Museum is at Ulverston, birthplace of Stan Laurel, the thinner half of the inimitable duo. The museum is crammed with films, tapes and all sorts of memorabilia.

Gothic splendour

The extravagantly twisted pillars of Holker Hall's dining room were carved in the 1870s by local craftsmen from oak trees growing on the Holker estate. Holker Hall, the grandest house in south Lakeland, is the family home of the Cavendishes. The Victorian front wing, built after a fire in 1874 destroyed part of the original seventeenth-century building, is open to the public.

Flocking together

In winter as many as 50,000 oystercatchers congregate in Morecambe Bay. They are easily recognisable by their natty black-and-white plumage and bright red bills. Instead of oysters, they eat the plentiful cockles along the shore.

Airborne wader

The plaintive cry of the curlew echoes along the south Cumbrian coastline where huge numbers of this large wader – mostly migrants from Scandinavia – gather to feed.

CROSSING THE SANDS

The beaches of Morecambe Bay are famously treacherous. The 120 square miles of sands revealed at low tide look smooth and golden, but they are riddled with hidden perils – quicksands, shifting river channels and a tidal bore which can rush up the Kent estuary as a two-metre wall of water.

Despite the dangers, for centuries travellers to and from the Lakes preferred to negotiate the seven miles of level sand from Hest Bank, near Lancaster, to Grange-over-Sands rather than the difficult twenty-mile mainland alternative. Guides were needed to lead the way, and in medieval times this was done by the monks of Cartmel and Conishead, but after the monasteries were closed the Crown took on responsibility for appointing guides.

The coming of the railway in 1857 put an end to the regular crossings of the sands, but to this day the Crown appoints its official guide. A fisherman living at Guide's Farm, Grange-over-Sands *(pictured below)*, still leads guided walks across the bay, marking the way with 'brobs', branches of laurel embedded in the ground – for centuries the method used to indicate safe routes across the sands.

WILD AND SPECTACULAR
LANDSCAPES – WESTERN LAKES AND COAST

Inland Cumbria's beauty is so spectacular that the coastline is often forgotten. But the sandy beaches are both beautiful and unspoilt, and dramatic St Bees Head forms the only stretch of high cliffs on the entire north-west coast of England. The towns of Whitehaven and Workington, which grew up with the coal and iron industries, still retain their Georgian heritage, and the Ravenglass to Eskdale railway, a relic of the iron industry, provides a scenic trip inland.

The western lakes have some of the most stunning landscapes of the region. Scafell Pike, England's highest point at 978 metres, towers above the valleys which radiate from it – Borrowdale, Buttermere, Ennerdale and Wasdale – each sheltering tranquil lakes in the hollows of its fells. Keswick, near northern Derwent Water, is the main centre for exploring the region.

Wide water

Crummock Water is separated from Buttermere by less than a mile, but its character is very different; it is wider and more open, without steep-sided mountains crowding along the shore. Wordsworth recommended the view from a boat at the centre of the lake: 'The scene is deep and solemn, and lonely; and in no other spot is the majesty of the Mountains so irresistibly felt as an omnipresence.'

White water

The best way to visit Stanley Force (left) is to take the Ravenglass–Eskdale railway as far as Dalegarth, then follow the two-mile trail which takes in the spectacular waterfall.

The lucky Penningtons

Descendants of the Pennington family have lived at the splendid Muncaster Castle since 1208. Legend has it that their succession is assured for as long as the famous 'Luck of Muncaster' – a fragile glass bowl given to the family by Henry VI – remains intact.

Alabaster angels

At Millom's Church of the Holy Trinity, angels adorn the alabaster tomb of a fifteenth-century lord of the manor, Sir Richard Hudleston, whose children are the tiny figures kneeling at the angels' feet. Norman Nicholson, Cumbria's most distinguished poet of recent years, lived in Millom all his life and is buried in Holy Trinity's graveyard.

A charming village

Woodsmoke hovers over the rooftops of Seatoller, one of five charming villages in the dramatic valley of Borrowdale; the others are Rosthwaite, Grange, Stonethwaite and Seathwaite. Seatoller's seventeenth-century whitewashed stone cottages were once quarry workers' homes.

The might of Rome

The Roman fort on Hardknott Pass perches eyrie-like above Eskdale. No one else has dared to dwell in this wild spot, and so the groundplan has survived intact.

Breakers on the shore

From the shingly beach just south of
Whitehaven, St Bees Head juts out into a rough
sea, forming Cumbria's westerly extremity.

Gems among the pebbles

The sandstone cliffs of St Bees Head loom large above
Fleswick Bay, an area favoured by stone hunters intent
upon discovering such rarities as carnelian, agate or jasper.

Inside the reactor

If you've ever wondered
what on earth it might be
like to be inside a nuclear
reactor, the Sellafield Visitor
Centre is the place to go.
Here in 'The Reactor' the
sensation is simulated
through a sound and light
film drama, one of many
exhibitions.

Unspoilt Ennerdale

With no public road running through it, lovely Ennerdale is one of the least visited of Lakeland valleys. From this western end of Ennerdale Water, there is little evidence of the large-scale conifer planting of the 1930s which some felt disfigured the upper reaches of the valley.

Pocklington's rock

This gigantic boulder in Borrowdale, a remnant of the last Ice Age, is known as the Bowder Stone. In Victorian times Joseph Pocklington drilled a hole in it, through which visitors could shake hands.

Classical elegance

St James's Church, Whitehaven, has the finest Georgian church interior in Cumbria. It was one of three churches built in Whitehaven in the eighteenth century to minister to the rapidly growing population. Before coal mines were sunk in the region, Whitehaven had been a tiny fishing village.

Tree-lined shores

Dusted with the late snows of spring, Fleetwith Fell rises precipitously from the tree-lined shores of Lake Buttermere. Only one-and-a-half miles long, this small stretch of water shares its valley with Crummock Water, and between the two lies the village of Buttermere, now a centre for exploring some of the grandest scenery in Cumbria.

Plumbago deliveries

This handsome 1954 delivery van once distributed the products of the Cumberland Pencil Company throughout Keswick but is now in the company's Pencil Museum. As long ago as the sixteenth century pencils – of a sort – were manufactured in Keswick from local deposits of graphite, or plumbago. The deposits are long since exhausted, but the industry still thrives, using graphite from the Far East.

Busy market

Visitors and locals rub shoulders at Keswick's busy Saturday market. Once a prosperous mining town and commercial centre, Keswick now depends heavily on the holiday trade. The church-like former town hall in the market square houses the tourist information centre.

Lonely road

Wasdale Head, at the north-eastern end of Wast Water, is one of the remotest spots in the Lake District. Looking down upon this isolated road – which takes climbers to the challenging rockfaces of Great Gable – is the conical peak of Yewbarrow.

Venerable stones

Castlerigg Stone Circle, east of Keswick, a group of some sixty standing stones dating from about 1400 BC, inspired Keats' description in *Hyperion* of 'a dismal cirque, Of Druid stones upon a forlorn moor'. Seen under the hazy skies of a June day, however, with an impressive backdrop of blue mountains rising in misty layers behind it, Castlerigg has an air of venerable and mysterious serenity.

From Cat Bells to Skiddaw

One of Cumbria's most famous views is from the top of the quaintly named Cat Bells. Variously described as a climb, a walk or – by that inveterate fell-walker Alfred Wainwright – an after-dinner stroll, the ascent is rewarded by stupendous views. Forming the backdrop to this splendour is Skiddaw, at 930 metres one of the four highest peaks in England. On the right in the distance is Blencathra, while Derwent Water's calm beauty is set off by several islands.

Windblown summits

*'On stern Blencathra's
perilous height
The winds are
tyrannous and strong'*

So wrote Coleridge about the mountain of Blencathra, or Saddleback, north-east of Keswick. The summit is indeed windy, but its ascent is gentle enough to encourage walkers, as the well-worn path along the ridge testifies.

Loweswater watering hole

The village of Loweswater and its pub, the Kirkstile, enjoy a magnificent setting midway between Loweswater and Crummock Water. Loweswater means 'leafy lake', which is particularly apt since the fellside on its southern shore is covered with trees.

The colonel's port

Maryport, at the mouth of the River Ellen on the west coast of
Cumbria, was created as a coal port by the eighteenth-
century lord of the manor, Colonel H Senhouse,
who named it after his wife, Mary. In its
nineteenth-century heyday Maryport was
a considerable shipbuilding centre, but
by the 1930s the coal pits had closed,
shipbuilding had ceased and the docks
were silting up. Today, however, the
port is being redeveloped as a small
boats' haven and the town has an
interesting maritime museum.

HOUND TRAILING

Dogs feature large in Lakeland life. Here fox-
hunting is a winter tradition, with sheepdog
trials and hound trailing taking over in summer.
The latter, variously described as canine fell
running or the Lakeland version of greyhound
racing, is a local speciality. The intensively
trained hounds are capable of impressive speed
and endurance over demanding terrain.

The principle is simple. A trail-layer pulls a
'drag' of sacking soaked in turpentine and aniseed
over the fells. The dogs are released and sprint
along, following the scent, avidly watched by the
crowd of bookies, spectators and owners in the
valley below. The sport is as popular as ever,
with sheepdog trials, agricultural shows or sports
meetings across the county staging one or more
hound trails as part of the entertainment.

TRADITIONAL BUILDINGS

Cumbria's typical building is the whitewashed stone cottage huddling against the mountain with its front to the hillside and its back to the view, an effective defence against wind and rain. Although a frequent sight now, there were few stone-built buildings in the county before the seventeenth century.

The cheapest and most abundant building material until then was wood; stone was expensive and so used for two main purposes: the glorification of God, and defence. The ruins of the great priories and abbeys, all built during the twelfth century, are in local stone, and few stately homes in the region are without a defensive, stonebuilt pele tower incorporated within the building.

But only when deforestation made wood a scarcer commodity did ordinary houses and cottages begin to be constructed from stone. In mountainous regions the local material was a coarse-grained slate, laid without the aid of mortar. Other features include whitewashed window alcoves to reflect light into the rooms, and interior walls panelled in wood to reduce draughts. Such cottages still stand, stout and weather resistant, a picturesque feature of the landscape.

Natural composition
The Barrow Beck, Ashness Bridge, Strutta Wood, Derwent Water and its mountain sentinel, Skiddaw, combine to compose a classic Lakeland view. The lane leads away from the lake to Watendlath, a remote hamlet only recently connected to mains electricity.

Looking south down the Newlands Valley from Swinside, near Keswick

THE HEART OF THE LAKE DISTRICT
CENTRAL LAKELAND

Sheer, rocky fells rising to majestic summits; lush green valleys, ancient woodlands and sheets of gleaming water; picturesque, hospitable towns and stone-built villages of great charm – it is all here in the heart of the Lake District.

Kendal, an attractive little town known as 'The Gateway to the Lakes', is perfectly complemented by the sublime scenery rising to the west. Most of the other towns cluster around the great lakes of Windermere and Coniston, with the smaller lakes dotted about nearby. This is the classic Lakeland that drew Wordsworth to Rydal and Grasmere, Ruskin to Brantwood on Coniston and Beatrix Potter to Near Sawrey by Esthwaite Water. From here a couple of roads lead northward through the high fells, yielding views unrivalled for sheer grandeur and spectacle. The more northerly lakes, Thirlmere, Ullswater and Haweswater, have a lonelier, bleaker beauty than those of the south.

A gentler beauty

This view from the southern end of Troutbeck of a calm and peaceful Windermere illustrates the gentler side of the Lakeland, with deciduous woodland, lush pasture and rolling – rather than soaring – fells.

Bird's-eye view

In the evening sun of early autumn all manner of boats stand out against the dark blue waters of Lake Windermere. In the extreme lower left the car ferry *Mallard* heads out of shot on its short journey from Bowness-on-Windermere to Far Sawrey. The ferry, half-way down the eleven-mile length of Lake Windermere, can save drivers a slow, if picturesque, round-trip of some twelve to fifteen miles.

Skiffs for hire

Elegant, varnished rowing-boats line the shore at Bowness. Thomas Hardy missed the coronation of George V, preferring to be in Cumbria, writing later that he got 'more satisfaction out of Coronation Day by spending it on Windermere than I would have done by spending it in a seat at the Abbey'.

Thriving centre

Since medieval times Kendal's prosperity has depended on wool: 'Kendal Green' was the cloth worn in Shakespeare's *Henry IV Part I*. The Georgian frontage of Farrer's coffee house was designed by Kendal architect Thomas Webster.

Five aisles and painted angels

Kendal's parish church, one of the largest in England, is most remarkable for its extraordinary width. Until the nineteenth century the walls were extravagantly painted; the ceiling of the north aisle still displays brightly painted angels.

BEATRIX POTTER

For those brought up on the tales of Beatrix Potter, a visit to Near Sawrey, a couple of miles from Hawkshead, will reveal familiar views at every turn. Potter owned Hill Top Farm here from 1905 until her death in 1943, and although it was never her permanent home, she wrote many books there, using the house, the garden and the surrounding area as inspiration for her famous illustrations.

She grew up in London, and it was only when she was in her late thirties, four years after the publication and success of *The Tale of Peter Rabbit*, that she bought Hill Top, using it as a place of solace and work after the death of her editor and fiancé, Norman Warne. There she continued to develop her keen interest in farming, building up her stock of Herdwick sheep, and keeping cows, pigs and poultry.

Store of ancient charm

The most photographed building in Ambleside, perhaps in Cumbria, Bridge House was built as a summerhouse and apple-store for nearby Ambleside Hall, which has since been demolished. The humble one-up one-down cottage, in the care of the National Trust, is now an information centre.

Hill Top, Near Sawrey

In 1909, in the course of buying a second farm in the village, she met the Hawkshead solicitor William Heelis, whom she married in 1912. As Beatrix Heelis, she threw herself into Lake District life, concentrating less on her books and more on farming. A keen conservationist, she was closely involved in the work of the National Trust, leaving at her death over 4,000 acres and fourteen farms in its care, ensuring that the land that she loved would be preserved for generations.

Beatrix Potter, outside Hill Top

A taste of Italy

Described as 'a perfect combination of the Venetian gondola and the English steam yacht', Coniston Water's *Gondola* provides a steam-powered service across the lake.

Solicitor's office

The Beatrix Potter Gallery in Hawkshead was once the office of Beatrix Potter's husband.

Along the Troutbeck valley

The village of Troutbeck is strung out along the western side of the Troutbeck valley some two-and-a-half miles north of Windermere. There are many fine seventeenth- and eighteenth-century houses, but the finest is probably Town End, a yeoman farmer's house dating from 1626 and now owned by the National Trust.

Britain's native squirrel

The native red squirrel still remains in sole possession of many Lakeland forests. Its immigrant rival, the grey squirrel, was introduced into this country in 1876 but has so far not managed to reach the remoter regions of Cumbria.

A home with a view

John Ruskin considered the view from his home, Brantwood, on the shores of Coniston Water, to be the best in Europe, which was lucky as he had bought the house without seeing it. During his years at Brantwood, from 1871 until his death in 1900, the great nineteenth-century art critic was an influential voice in social affairs and, as one of the first true 'conservationists', helped inspire the formation of the National Trust. The house, open to the public and containing an extensive collection of Ruskin's papers and possessions, is a fascinating testimony to this Victorian 'Renaissance man'.

Man of wood

Deep in Grizedale Forest stands the figure of the Ancient Forester, constructed by David Kemp, and one of the many exhibits on the forest's nine-mile sculpture trail.

King of the skies

In the heart of the fells you may just see a golden eagle soaring majestically above. Absent for 200 years, a few of these rare birds returned to Cumbria in 1969, the only wild breeding pairs in England; consequently their nest sites are closely guarded.

Rydal, near Ambleside

The River Rothay flows from Grasmere through Rydal (here) and into Lake Windermere.

Lanty Slee's distillery

Fell Foot Farm is the last habitation on the lonely road from Little Langdale to the bleak Wrynose Pass. The valley was the haunt of the legendary nineteenth-century smuggler, Lanty Slee, and it was at this farm that he kept his distilleries and illicit whisky. The scenery surrounding Little Langdale is that of the high fells, and the views in all directions are breathtaking.

Whooper swan's winter home

Elter Water, one of the smallest lakes, lies at the mouth of the Langdale valley. Behind are the imposing twin peaks of the Langdale Pikes: on the left is Pike of Stickle and on the right Harrison Stickle. The lake's name derives from the Norse for 'swan lake', and on occasion whooper swans do indeed spend the winter here.

Twin peaks

Above the smooth glaciated floor of Great Langdale valley, the Langdale Pikes crouch like lions. Wordsworth described the mountains as lusty twins 'echoing back in the grim and breathless hour of noon, the thunder's greeting'. They dominate the scenery in this serenely beautiful region of central Lakeland, a walkers' paradise with few buildings other than the occasional lonely farm or climbers' hut.

CUMBRIAN SPORTS

The traditional sports of Cumbria – fell running, hound trailing, sheepdog trials, even Lakeland wrestling – are clearly linked with farming and mountains. Rearing sheep on the hills fostered wiry physiques possessed of great stamina, tested by races up and down the fells. The threat to lambs posed by foxes has ensured that Lakeland hounds are among the finest in the country.

While foxhounds rest in the summer, trail hounds race over set courses, and sheepdogs, faithfully following instructions, swap the bleak, winter fells for green fields fringed by spectators.

Lakeland wrestling was once carried out on the exposed fell range named High Street, but has now moved down to the valley shows. These are held at a variety of venues, but most famously at Grasmere and Ambleside. All manner of Cumbrian sports are celebrated at the shows – from Egremont Crab Fair's gurning (or face-pulling) to Wasdale Head's competition for the biggest liar.

Small home for a great man

William Wordsworth was already famous when in 1799 he came to live at Dove Cottage in Grasmere. Seldom has so eminent a man – not to mention sister, wife, three children and frequent visitors – lived in so small an abode. Dating from 1617, the building had only just ceased to be a pub when Wordsworth moved in with his sister. It is furnished as it was then, with the original furniture and the bedroom papered with newspapers.

Creative siblings

Wordsworth believed Dove Cottage to be 'the loveliest spot that man hath ever found', and his years here resulted in his 'golden decade'. *The Prelude (left)* contains some of his greatest poetry, while his sister Dorothy's meticulous daily journal *(right)* offers a fascinating counterpoint.

Wordsworth's last home

Rydal Mount became Wordsworth's home after his appointment in 1813 to the sinecure of Distributor of Stamps in Westmorland gave him a new-found affluence. Here he spent his last years, now a famous man. Much of the house is as he left it, but his most visible legacy is the four-acre garden he created.

'Public highway'

Seven-mile-long Ullswater is the second largest lake, snaking along from Glenridding in the south-west to Pooley Bridge in the north-east. The famous Ullswater steamers ply its length, stopping at Howtown on their journey from one end to the other. Anyone can launch a boat on the lake for it is officially classified as a public highway; the speed limit is 10 mph. The main view is from Glencoyne; the inset picture is from the shore just north of Glenridding, looking north-east past Norfolk Island.

THE CAMPBELLS AND CONISTON

In August 1939, just before the outbreak of war, Sir Malcolm Campbell took his speedboat *Bluebird* on to Coniston Water and set a new world water speed record at 141.74 mph. After the war his son Donald took over and between 1956 and 1959 set five new records, the last at 276.33 mph. Eight years on he and a dedicated team were back on Coniston Water determined to reach 300 mph. On the morning of 4 January 1967, after weeks of delays caused by bad weather, he started the vast jet engine of the new *Bluebird*. On his second run – his first had skimmed Coniston at 297 mph – the boat reared fifteen metres into the air and crashed into the water, sending up walls of spray. *Bluebird* sank into forty metres of water; Donald Campbell's body has never been found.

Donald Campbell

Bluebird *on Coniston Water, shortly before it crashed in 1967*

THE BORDER LANDS
CARLISLE, HADRIAN'S WALL AND THE NORTH PENNINES

In the second century AD the Roman Emperor Hadrian built his seventy-six-mile-long wall to protect the northern outpost of the Roman Empire from the warlike peoples of Scotland. From then until the eighteenth century, the disputed border lands around Hadrian's Wall were a scene of strife and turmoil. Carlisle, Cumbria's capital, has been shaped by these conflicts: its great castle, stout city walls, ancient cathedral and fascinating museum all have stories to tell.

Much of the land which changed hands over the centuries was the lush Solway Plain, west of Carlisle. This rises gradually as it follows the valley of the River Irthing inland to the wild heights of the north Pennines. Here, bald, open moorland criss-crossed by winding sheep tracks and gouged by fast-flowing streams offers superb walking country: the Pennine Way mounts steadily to the summit of Cross Fell before leaving Cumbria at the dramatic waterfall of Caldron Snout.

Heavenly workmanship

Carlisle Cathedral's choir is one of the loveliest in England. The fabulous ceiling, spangled with stars and studded by ornate roof-bosses, has supports for a hammerbeam roof, each with a golden angel astride it, but owing to a change of plan on the part of the builders, no beams were ever installed.

Red sandstone and old glass

Set between pinnacled buttresses and flanked by statues of the apostles, Carlisle Cathedral's magnificent east window is its chief glory, and perhaps the finest in the land. A triumph of fourteenth-century stonework, the window contains 600-year-old glass in its upper tracery.

Creative doomed men

Condemned prisoners held in Carlisle Castle in the fifteenth century carved elaborate designs on the sandstone walls.

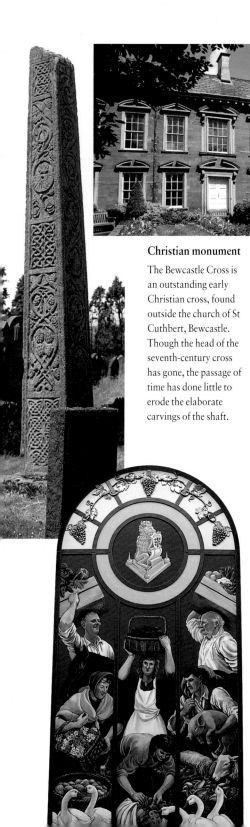

Christian monument

The Bewcastle Cross is an outstanding early Christian cross, found outside the church of St Cuthbert, Bewcastle. Though the head of the seventh-century cross has gone, the passage of time has done little to erode the elaborate carvings of the shaft.

History distilled

Carlisle's museum is based in Tullie House, a fine Jacobean mansion. Its displays on the history of Carlisle include exhibits on the Romans and the border reivers.

BORDER RAIDERS

For 400 years, from the fourteenth to the seventeenth century, almost all Cumbria was prey to marauding, lawless raiders or 'reivers'. The exception was the most mountainous heart of the Lake District which was too remote and too poor to interest the raiders. Exploiting the near-anarchy of the border area, they would leave their native Scotland and return with cattle, sheep and any valuables they could carry.

The Cumbrians' response was to build pele towers with redoubtable defences to withstand the attacks by formidable Scots families. Pele towers are now often incorporated into stately homes or used as farm buildings. Another product of these lawless times is the ballads written by the English, poignant tales of grief and loss. These can be heard at the Tullie House museum in Carlisle, where the times of the reivers are excellently recaptured.

Carlisle's warlike face

Carlisle's nineteenth-century citadel guards the southern approach to the city. William Lowther, whose statue fronts the Citadel, was a member of a powerful Cumbrian family.

The edge of the civilised world

The stone blocks of Hadrian's Wall from the Solway Firth to the Tyne form an impressive barrier across the Pennines. Begun in AD 120 by Emperor Hadrian, the wall marked the limit of Roman conquest, protecting the subjugated lands from the barbarians to the north. Here at Birdoswald are the remains of the Roman camp of Camboglanna.

A bright future

This colourful mural is part of the award-winning Lanes shopping precinct in Carlisle. The complex, built in 1982, replaces an area of narrow streets and dilapidated houses and shops known as the Lanes. The new shops' facades are designed to imitate the earlier buildings.

Green and pleasant lands

Enclosed by the mountains of southern Scotland, Northumberland and Cumbria, the Solway Plain is a rich, fertile area drained by the tributaries of the rivers Eden and Esk flowing west towards the Solway Firth. Here, near the village of Banks, the peaceful green valley of the River Irthing is, like much of the region, productive dairy and stock-rearing country.

In the heart of the mountains

Alston is perched about 300 metres above sea level, and its streets slope precipitously up from the River Nent, with old grey houses clinging precariously to the steep pavements. The Pennine Way leads through the town on its 256-mile, high-altitude journey down the backbone of England, starting at Kirk Yetholm, just into Scotland, and ending at Edale in Derbyshire.

Pointer to the past

Deep in one of the remotest corners of all Cumbria is Garrigill, a village close to the high Pennine sources of the rivers Nent and South Tyne. The area was for many years the centre of lead and zinc mining.

England's highest waterfall

High in the Pennines the River Tees tumbles a spectacular 60 metres, part of a rock staircase some 140 metres long. Known as Caldron Snout, this mighty waterfall, the highest in England, forms the boundary between Cumbria, to the left, and Durham, to the right.

Lanercost Priory

Many of the great stones used to build Lanercost Priory came from nearby Hadrian's Wall, built a thousand years earlier. The priory's demise came in 1536 with the dissolution of the monasteries, but the north aisle of the priory's church, with its fine west front, remains intact.

Where hedgerows will not grow

Typical of the north Pennines – and indeed of all upland Cumbria – are drystone walls. Built of local rock, they are usually made of granite, slate or limestone, and are remarkably robust. Made without mortar, they can last for 200 years or more. Many drystone walls date from the early nineteenth century, when the Napoleonic Wars forced up the price of foodstuffs, so encouraging farmers to enclose land previously thought too poor to be viable.

$\mathcal{E}$DEN'S GREEN VALE – THE EDEN VALLEY

$\mathcal{S}$andwiched between the Pennines and the Lakeland peaks is the valley of the River Eden, a suitably paradisiacal name for this fertile and lovely stretch of countryside which begins in the Yorkshire Dales and extends through the heart of Cumbria. The deep rich red of the valley's soil contrasts with the green of its meadows and woodlands, and the local red sandstone is a striking feature of many of the region's towns and villages.

Historic Appleby, picturesque Kirkby Stephen and the delightful villages of Kirkoswald and Armathwaite cluster along the banks of the Eden, while Penrith, the main commercial centre, is sited closer to one of the Eden's tributaries, the Eamont. The land was settled in prehistoric times and today the valley is dotted with ancient churches and great houses, many well fortified against border raids, and castles tell of the families who have shaped the region's history over many centuries.

Fertile valley
After the rocky heights of Cumbria's fells, a gentle stroll in the Eden Valley may come as a relaxing change. Beginning its course high up in the Yorkshire Dales, the Eden meanders north and west to its mouth at the Solway Firth, skirting the east of the Cumbrian Mountains.

Witches of stone
On a lonely spot surrounded by bleak hills and overlooking the Eden Valley, a ring of prehistoric stones stands sharply against the sky. Consisting of one rakishly positioned five-metre stone surrounded by a ring of smaller boulders, Long Meg and her Daughters is the third largest circle in Britain.

Lady Anne's monuments

At Appleby-in-Westmorland, two white pillars, each surmounted by a golden sundial, stand at either end of Boroughgate, the town's main street. The columns were erected by Lady Anne Clifford who in the seventeenth century married the Earl of Pembroke, owner of Appleby Castle.

Striking frontage

Dalemain is built around a medieval pele tower, which is now home to a museum for the Westmorland and Cumberland Yeomanry. But the most striking feature of Dalemain is the nine-bay frontage added by Edward Hasell in the 1740s. The Hasell family lives there still.

A former queen

In the days when the county still existed, Temple Sowerby used to style itself the 'queen of Westmorland villages'. Its name derives from the Knights Templar, past owners of the village.

Cathedral in miniature

The attractive twelfth-century church of St Lawrence in Crosby Ravensworth has been likened to a cathedral on a small scale. Surrounded by old trees near the River Lyvennet, it is the high point of a pleasant village.

SETTLE–CARLISLE RAILWAY

It is often said of this monumental example of Victorian civil engineering that it simply should never have been built. Hundreds of navvies lost their lives as the line made hesitant progress through some of England's harshest terrain, while the financial costs leapt ahead at breakneck speed. But a combination of stubbornness and a not entirely misplaced belief that the new route to Scotland could be profitable ensured that on 1 May 1876, some seven years after construction began, the first passenger train hauled itself up the 'Long Drag' and over the north Pennines.

In building this line the Midland Railway Company created one of the finest railway journeys in the world. The Cumbrian stretch from Dent Head north to Carlisle contains some of the most spectacular and bleakest scenery. Ais Gill, at 356 metres, is the high point of this, the highest main line in England. From here the descent follows the infant Eden beneath Wild Boar Fell and into the gentler Eden Valley. After Appleby the line crosses pleasant agricultural land to its terminus at Carlisle.

Viaduct near Kirkby Stephen

A grand entrance

The brown-and-white porticoed arcades of this building in Kirkby Stephen have an air of civic dignity about them, resembling the entrance to a station, market place or even town hall. But this is, in fact, the gateway to the thirteenth-century church of St Stephen.

The church, one of the largest and most magnificent in Cumbria, contains some splendid tombs.

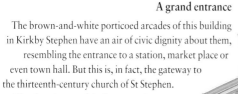

Undisturbed prayer

The ruins of Shap Abbey stand in remote countryside beside the River Lowther. The abbey was founded in the twelfth century by the Premonstratensian Order, or White Canons, who were keen to find an isolated spot suitable for contemplation and prayer. The West Tower, the most extensive of the ruins, was built c.1500.

Red stones of Penrith

The ruins of Penrith's fourteenth-century castle are built of the distinctive blood-red local stone. Penrith itself has been a market town since the Middle Ages and is full of traditional shops. Its week still revolves around its Tuesday market.

Sham castle

Despite appearances to the contrary, Fort Putnam is not a battle-scarred medieval fortress but rather a humble farmhouse. It is one of three extraordinary farms built by the eleventh Duke of Norfolk on his vast estate at Greystoke. All three were named after American revolutionary heroes.

Formidable defences

The forbidding Norman keep dominates Appleby Castle, which in turn dominates the little town clustered round its walls. The castle's impressive defences were built to withstand the onslaughts of the Scots, who actually managed to capture it in 1388. During the Civil War, Lady Anne Clifford, an ardent Royalist, fortified and held the castle for three years.

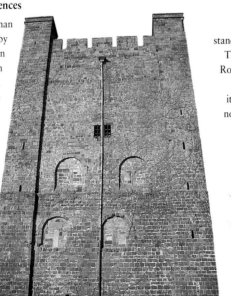

Sentinel-like castle

The cracked, weatherbeaten shell of Brough Castle stands sentinel-like beside an equally stricken ancient tree. The Norman castle was built on the earlier remains of a Roman fort, and was restored by Lady Anne Clifford in the seventeenth century. Now a picturesque ruin, it stands in lovely countryside at the foot of the north Pennines, close to the River Swindale, and has magnificent views of the Eden Valley.

*G*ENTLE DALES AND CRAGGY HEIGHTS

THE DALES

A small part of the Yorkshire Dales National Park lies within Cumbria: the westernmost edge, containing Garsdale, on the main east–west route through the Dales, and lovely Dentdale. One of the smallest of the national park's dales, Dentdale is also one of the prettiest – a patchwork of sloping green fields with the barren heights of Rise Hill and Crag Hill looming on either side. The delightful whitewashed village of Dent can be found halfway up the valley. At the bottom of Dentdale lies Sedbergh, a small grey town nestling at the foot of the green, rounded hummocks of the Howgill Fells.

East of the Howgills the characteristic limestone scenery of the Dales begins in earnest. The craggy escarpments of Wild Boar Fell, towering over the upper reaches of the Eden Valley (known here as Mallerstang), and the huge flat-topped Baugh Fell are as dramatic as any of Yorkshire's peaks further to the east.

Rounded fells

The bare, rounded tops of the Howgill Fells, dusted in snow, rise up from the small Dales town of Sedbergh. Despite the fact that they reach 676 metres at their highest point, the Howgills' relative proximity to the sea at Morecambe Bay ensures that snow rarely stays for long.

Whitewash and cobbles

In the south-eastern corner of Cumbria and within the Yorkshire Dales National Park lies the attractive village of Dent. Cobbled streets and whitewashed houses lend it something of the air of a Cornish fishing village, though the spectacular scenery all around is clearly northern.

Wild Boar Fell

The distinctive flat top of Wild Boar Fell lies on the western side of the valley of the young River Eden, here known as Mallerstang. The cairns mark the 708-metre summit of Wild Boar Fell, apparently so called as it is where the last wild boar in England was killed. The mountain's eastern foot is skirted for several miles by the Settle–Carlisle railway.

Source of the Eden

The characteristic limestone escarpments of the Dales rise bleakly above Mallerstang, close to the source of the River Eden. The ancient-sounding name of this lonely valley is from the Welsh word *moel* (bare hill) and the old Norse *stong* (boundary stone).

Arthurian romance

Despite many attempts by the Clifford family to rebuild Pendragon Castle, just south of Kirkby Stephen, time has finally achieved what the Scots raiders could not, and reduced the much-restored Norman fortress to a picturesque ruin. The castle's evocative name is probably a reference to Uther Pendragon, father of the legendary King Arthur, and may have been chosen because according to an ancient myth he built a castle somewhere in the region.

Former knitting centre

In the past, Sedbergh's economy depended upon the domestic knitting trade, with local sheep providing the raw material. At the top of Finkle Street, shown here, there were once several spinning galleries where the yarn was spun; one of these galleries still exists.

THE DALES

Unchanged market town

The delightful market town of Kirkby Lonsdale lies to the south-east of Kendal. Its old squares, pretty streets and eighteenth-century houses have changed little since Bonnie Prince Charlie passed through the town in 1745, and its church is the best-known example of Norman religious architecture in Cumbria.

Ruskin's View

J M W Turner painted the River Lune from this vantage point near Kirkby Lonsdale. His friend John Ruskin was so impressed that he sought out the spot and wrote of it 'I do not know in all my own country . . . a place more naturally divine'.

The work of the devil?

Kirkby Lonsdale's three-arched Devil's Bridge is thought to be about 700 years old, the name apparently deriving from a legend which claims that the devil built it in a single night. Rarely has he been so beneficent! Both the old and new bridges cross the beautiful River Lune, which flows down the western edge of the Pennines. The devil also thoughtfully elected to fill the pool beneath his bridge with salmon.

Rise Hill

Even in early summer when the meadows on the lower slopes of Deepdale, in the foreground, and Dentdale, in the background, are lush with hay and buttercups, the long, brooding mass of Rise Hill remains grey and barren. It forms an impenetrable barrier between Dentdale and Garsdale, a few miles to the north.

WALKING IN THE DALES

For some who visit England's mountainous north-west corner, driving along country lanes is as close as they wish to come to the scenery. Others are not satisfied until they are walking the high fells, and for these there is no finer county than Cumbria.

Many of Lakeland's walks are rightly well-known, but Cumbria's corner of the Yorkshire Dales can also claim some superb walks. The Dales Way is a particularly good means of exploring this little-visited area. Beginning at Ilkley in West Yorkshire and following a mainly low-level route, it enters Cumbria near the Dent Head Viaduct and

Dent Head Viaduct

goes downhill nearly all the way until the foothills of the Lakeland fells are reached near Bowness, the end of the eighty-one-mile waymarked walk. Some of England's most beautiful valleys are followed, including glorious Dentdale and a stretch of the Lune valley near Sedbergh.

Hikers at the Sun Inn, Dent

- Bewcastle
- Birdoswald
- *Hadrian's Wall*
- *Lanercost Priory*
- **Carlisle**
- Alston
- Garrigill
- Kirkoswald
- *Cross Fell* △
- *Long Meg and her Daughters*
- Maryport
- *River Derwent*
- *Bassenthwaite Lake*
- Caldron Snout
- Workington
- Skiddaw △
- △ *Blencathra*
- Greystoke
- **Penrith**
- Temple Sowerby
- *Dalemain*
- Appleby
- *River Eden*
- **Keswick**
- *Derwent Water*
- *Castlerigg Stone Circle*
- *Lowther Park*
- Brough
- Loweswater
- *Cat Bells* △
- *Bowder Stone*
- *Ullswater*
- Crummock Water
- Whitehaven
- Buttermere
- Rosthwaite
- Stonethwaite
- Seatoller
- *Thirlmere*
- *Hawes Water*
- *Shap Abbey*
- Crosby Ravensworth
- Kirkby Stephen
- Ennerdale Water
- Seathwaite
- St Bees
- Sellafield
- *Wasdale*
- *Wast Water*
- Grasmere
- *Rydal Mount*
- *Rydal*
- Pendragon Castle
- *Howgill Fells*
- *Wild Boar Fell*
- *Scafell Pike*
- *Elter Water*
- Langdale
- **Ambleside**
- Eskdale
- *Hardknott*
- *Tarn Hows*
- Troutbeck
- Hawkshead
- **Windermere**
- Ravenglass
- *Stanley Force*
- Coniston
- **Bowness**
- *Muncaster Castle*
- *Brantwood*
- *Grizedale Forest*
- *Lake Windermere*
- **Kendal**
- Sedbergh
- *Dentdale*
- Ulpha
- *Coniston Water*
- △ *Cartmel Fell*
- *Sizergh Castle*
- *Levens Hall*
- Dent
- Millom
- *Cartmel Priory*
- Grange-over-Sands
- Kirkby Lonsdale
- Haverigg
- Ulverston
- Askam in Furness
- *Holker Hall*
- Arnside
- *Furness Abbey*
- *Bardsea Country Park*
- Barrow-in-Furness
- Walney Island
- *Morecambe Bay*
- *Piel Castle*
- *CUMBRIAN MOUNTAINS*
- *BORROWDALE*